IMAGES
of America

GLENS FALLS

THE FEEDER CANAL, C. THE 1880S. When the canal opened in 1832, commerce between Glens Falls and points south developed rapidly. Limestone, marble, and lumber were shipped to New York City. Coal and produce from New York City ports were returned. The men who financed the canal also owned the mills along the river, the canal boats, and wood lots in the Adirondacks. Millionaires were made in Glens Falls.

IMAGES
of America

GLENS FALLS

Gwen Palmer, Bob Bayle,
and Stan Malecki

ARCADIA
PUBLISHING

Published by Arcadia Publishing
Charleston, South Carolina

Library of Congress Catalog Card Number: 2004107304

For all general information contact Arcadia Publishing at:
Telephone 843-853-2070
Fax 843-853-0044
E-mail sales@arcadiapublishing.com
For customer service and orders:
Toll-Free 1-888-313-2665

Visit us on the Internet at www.arcadiapublishing.com

THE KEENAN LIME COMPANY, C. 1880. Limestone quarrying was done manually near the Feeder Canal and the Hudson River. Poles and pulleys moved large slabs of rock onto wagons that took them to the canal for transport. While quarrymen work, a well-dressed audience on the ledge is entertained by the activity.

CONTENTS

ACKNOWLEDGMENTS

Special recognition is given to the Corners Project of the Chapman Historical Museum. The project grew from an idea presented by the then Adirondack Community College professor Kilmer Heighton to place the history of the city on the Internet. Meetings were held among Chapman staff, community leaders, teachers, and other volunteers to discuss the merits of such a project. Because of its daunting possibilities, the project moved slowly until a grant was received from the North Hudson Electronic Education Empowerment Project to fund a computer, printer, scanner, and a digital camera. Educator Robin Wright stepped forward to assemble a group of interested volunteers. With the complete dedication of Gwen Palmer and Bob Bayle, the project came to fruition. Peter Trumbull and the staff of the Chapman Historical Museum provided additional help.

Using the archives at the museum, Glens Falls City Hall, the Warren County Building, and the Queensbury Town Hall, a corps of volunteers began searching deeds and other records for the history of the city's streets and buildings. This information was used to create the Corners link on the Chapman Historical Museum's Web site at www.chapmanmuseum.org.

During research, volunteers realized that the museum archives held a wealth of photographs depicting the community's roots. Because Arcadia Publishing's Images of America series was sold in the museum gift shop, the idea to assemble and publish a photographic history of Glens Falls took hold.

Special thanks must be given to Timothy Weidner, director of the Chapman Historical Museum, for making its archives available. Along the way, museum staff members Laura Van Guilder and Sandra Baker gave assistance. Museum volunteers Lillian Casola, Robin Wright, and Dr. Margarethe McCurry provided additional help. Special appreciation goes to the family and friends of Corners Project volunteers Gwen Palmer, Bob Bayle, and Stan Malecki, whose support for their work has made it a labor of love. Recognition goes to Theodore Beaudet, the Francis Bayle photograph collection, and Thomas Curran, who loaned special photographs.

INTRODUCTION

The city of Glens Falls has gone through many changes since the time it was a settlement referred to as the Corners. During the tumult of the French and Indian and Revolutionary Wars, early Quaker settlers abandoned their homes and moved to the safety of Connecticut, then slowly returned to their homes when the fighting was over. With the tremendous Hudson River waterpower available at the falls for running mills, people settled near its shores.

By the late 1700s, the village became known as Wing's Falls, named after Abraham Wing, an early Quaker settler. Through the settling of some debts, tradition has it, ownership of the name was transferred to Johannes Glenn and the village name changed to Glenn's Falls. The village was incorporated on April 12, 1839. In later years, the Glens Falls Insurance Company dropped the apostrophe, and the present use of "Glens Falls" began.

In 1839, the village board appropriated money to dig wells, build cisterns, and buy pumps, ladders, hooks, and other equipment to establish fire protection. In 1842, the first volunteer fire department was organized as the Glens Falls Fire Company No. 1. Additional wells and cisterns were created to expand the system in 1861 and were used until 1873, when a community water system was established. Fire stations existed on Ridge Street next to the present city hall, on South Street next to the Madden Hotel, on Warren Street, and on Elm Street.

The police department began with the election of a lone constable in 1839, when the village was incorporated. The community had existed for 75 years without any law enforcement, but people viewed law and order differently at the time. For 21 years, beginning in 1839, only 12 constables were elected. For four years, none were elected due to the lack of funding for the position.

With the community's proximity to the Adirondacks, the logging industry brought much wealth to Glens Falls. The men who owned the wood lots also owned the many mills built along this stretch of the Hudson River. Later, when the Champlain Canal was built east of town, the Feeder Canal was developed to control water levels in the locks. With the advent of the canal (financed by the same men), lumber, limestone, black marble, and cement from the mills could be shipped to New York City. Coal and other consumable products were then shipped back to Glens Falls. The mill owners also owned the boats used on the canal; the rich therefore got richer, and by the mid-1800s, Glens Falls was home to many millionaires. This wealth contributed to the economic, cultural, and social development of the village and, later, the city.

While the wealthy built mansions with luxurious gardens along the village's main streets, the workers set down roots in other parts of town. Most residents had large vegetable gardens and traveled by horse and buggy. Stables, carriage houses, and barns existed throughout the village. There was no electricity or indoor plumbing, so even the richest families had to rely on outhouses, candles, and oil lamps. When the Glens Falls Gas and Light Company was formed in 1854, people living in the village soon found themselves lighting their homes with gas. They found that extra cleaning was required, however, to remove the soot that accumulated on walls and ceilings. Electricity was first used in a sawmill and for streetlights in 1880. A few homes had electricity by 1884, but lighting with gas was more common in homes until 1923. Telephones were first introduced in 1879 with 55 phones serviced by one day and one night operator working at the Times Building, now called the Colvin Building, on Glen Street.

From 1848 to 1904, a "plank road" ran from Glens Falls to Lake George. Stagecoaches ran between the two communities regularly, but service slowed dramatically after the railroad extended to the lake. Rail service began in 1869, when a station opened on Maple Street, opposite Oak Street. The building was moved to a new site facing Locust Street in 1897 on the same side of Maple. A second station was built on the corners of Lawrence and Cooper Streets in 1897. Passenger service to Glens Falls ended in 1958. By 1885, an active trolley line connected Glens Falls with Sandy Hill (Hudson Falls) and Fort Edward. Horses pulled the first cars. On June 14, 1891, the first electricity-powered cars arrived, and by 1897 eighteen cars operated on more than 10 1/2 miles of track.

On November 23, 1900, a hospital opened in the donated home of Solomon Parks on Park Street. The hospital had beds for 22 patients, as well as six private rooms. The hospital quickly outgrew this space, however, and a three-story building with rooms for 72 patients was built at the corner of Basin and Park Streets, opening on December 7, 1910. A school for nurses was established in 1903, and it moved into the original building when the new hospital was finished. The building remained a school until 1932.

In 1908, the New York State legislature passed a charter for the formation of the city of Glens Falls. This book has been designed as a pictorial history of Glens Falls's roots as a community, and to give readers a greater appreciation of the city's past.

One

THE RIVER

THE COVERED BRIDGE, 1842–1890. The covered bridge was built to replace a rickety "free" bridge that was determined to be unsafe. Warren and Saratoga Counties each received $2,500 from New York State toward the destruction of the old bridge. Warren County awarded $1,500 to build the new span. At first there was no center support underneath, but in 1886 the bridge began to settle in the middle as much as one foot, so a stone pier was built. The logs were left by receding water when the spring deluge stopped. If a covered bridge had no snow on its surface to allow sleighs to cross in winter, snow had to be shoveled onto the bridge in order to allow travel by vehicles with runners on them.

THE COVERED BRIDGE, 1869. The latticework of the covered bridge allowed light to enter the otherwise dark tunnel. The walls were used for commercial and political posters. The boards were pinned together. Constructed of white ash, the poles and crosspieces used to strengthen the center of the bridge were washed away twice during its existence. Visible in this photograph are hanging support poles that are loosened from their moorings.

A SPRING FLOOD, 1869. During one of the many spring floods, buildings along the river were washed away. The submerged building on the left is what remains of one of the first mills on the river, the Abraham Wing Mill. It was incorporated into the Finch Pruyn property but was lost in this flood. As with any disaster, an audience finds the crisis fascinating.

THE GLENS FALLS LIME WORKS, C. 1880. Limestone deposits are ubiquitous in the area along the Hudson River. Limestone was used as a building material and was also ground to a powder to be used in the making of cement. The two steeples in the background are from the Presbyterian and Catholic churches on Warren Street.

THE LUMBERYARDS, C. THE LATE 1800S. The Finch Pruyn Company produced cut lumber that was stacked and transported to cities along the lower Hudson River. The Feeder Canal, which bypasses the falls in the river, allowed boats to meet the Champlain Canal and the Hudson on its way south. Piers for sorting logs are visible in the river near the stacked lumber.

THE FINCH PRUYN QUARRIES, C. 1900. Before Finch Pruyn became famous for its paper production, it was known for its quarrying. Limestone and black marble prove to be economically beneficial to the company and the community. The tower and tank of the Glens Falls Gasworks are visible beyond the bridge to the right.

THE GLENS FALLS GASWORKS, C. 1890. The gasworks was built in 1854 at the corner of Basin and Canal Streets. Coal shipped via the Hudson River, Champlain Canal, and finally the Feeder Canal was used in the production of gas that needed to be purified before being sent into the system of mains. By 1923, there were 53 miles of gas mains serving 4,443 meters in Glens Falls.

THE SAWMILL, C. 1895. Finch Pruyn was one of the first mills on the Hudson River. Black marble and limestone were quarried on the site, and a lumbermill soon followed. The company existed on both sides of the bridge, and lumberyards were located on the west side. In this image, logs can be seen on the left while cut lumber is piled on wagons and on the ground near the barns. Part of the Iron Bridge is visible.

A LOGJAM, C. 1895. Each spring, 13-foot logs were sent down the Hudson River from the Adirondacks to the mills in Glens Falls. High water, however, often caused the logs to end up in locations other than where they were expected. This jam is west of the Route 9 Iron Bridge on Finch Pruyn property.

COOPER'S CAVE, 1890. Cooper's Cave became famous from its inclusion in the book *The Last of the Mohicans*, by James Fenimore Cooper. Area families picnic here and enjoy the peace and tranquility of the location. This photograph is unusual in that the photographer is inside the cave, shooting out. Notice the man leaning against the limestone wall on the left of the photograph. The boys are sitting on logs left behind from the spring log run.

COOPER'S CAVE, C. 1870. In 1824, James Fenimore Cooper visited the area and observed the cave from the bridge over the falls in the Hudson River. The cave became famous for its role in *The Last of the Mohicans*. It is actually not a cave, but rather an eroded passageway in the limestone rock. In this photograph, taken c. 1870, a gentleman enjoys the solitude of the cave along with logs left over from the spring drive. The cave was open to visitors until 1961.

THE IRON BRIDGE, C. 1890. Workers on the girders in this image indicate that the bridge was still under construction. In this view facing the Glen Street hill, the spire of the Presbyterian church on Warren Street is visible. The trolley system was in development in Glens Fall at this time, but tracks were not yet on the bridge. This bridge was destroyed during a spring flood in 1913. Here, a child is enjoying a ride in the back of a wagon.

THE IRON BRIDGE, 1900. Built in 1890, the Iron Bridge replaced the covered bridge of 1842–1890. The Iron Bridge saw Glens Falls through a period of tremendous growth. The stone pier under the bridge was left over from the covered bridge that needed added support for its sagging middle section. The buildings on the right belong to the Finch Pruyn Company.

A LOG DRIVE, C. 1915. The Hudson River was a cheap source of transportation for the Adirondack lumber companies to bring their logs to the mills in Glens Falls. Large booms of thick logs and chains formed floating corrals to be used to help separate identified logs for delivery at the appropriate sites. Stone-filled piers allowed workers to use pike poles for moving the logs.

RIVER PIERS, C. 1900. Large piers were constructed in the Hudson River to allow men to sort logs according to ownership. Piers were filled with large rocks to prevent moving logs from destroying the man-made "islands." Since the Iron Bridge is visible here, this picture was taken between 1890 and 1913. Logs are shown separated by large "booms" floating in the river.

THE HUDSON RIVER, 1899. The Iron Bridge crossed the Hudson River. The arch under the bridge was actually on the South Glens Falls side of the river but became the symbol of the Glens Falls Insurance Company. A terra-cotta version of the arch hung over the company's entrance. The building was sold and the terra-cotta piece removed; it now hangs in the entrance foyer to the Chapman Historical Museum.

THE FLOOD OF MARCH 27, 1913. At 4:30 in the afternoon, people gathered to watch the rising water in the Hudson River. Clearly, the bridge was in jeopardy. This view faces south, and the people are standing alongside the Feeder Canal. At 9:55 that evening, the bridge was swept away into the roiling chasm of water. All connections with South Glens Falls were broken.

THE FOOTBRIDGE, 1913. When the Iron Bridge went out in the spring flood of March 27, 1913, connections with South Glens Falls were cut off. A footbridge was quickly built and used until a loaned railroad bridge was put in place as a temporary crossway. The water from the Hudson River still poured over the rock formations.

NEW YORK TELEPHONE WORKERS, 1913. When the Iron Bridge was destroyed in the flood of 1913, trolley, electric, and telephone service to South Glens Falls was interrupted. Telephone workers were called into service with their horses and wagons. The company logo (NYTCo) appears on the side of two wagons and is being held by a man on the far left wagon near the fence by the Feeder Canal.

THE QUEENSBURY-MOREAU VIADUCT, C. 1917. The steel bridge collapsed into the Hudson River in 1913, and a new concrete bridge was begun. The viaduct, which cost approximately $150,000, opened in 1915. The new bridge allowed for the approaches at either end to be graded so that they were not nearly as steep to enter. Trolleys and horse-drawn carriages traveled across the brick-lined bridge.

A SPIRAL STAIRCASE, C. 1917. When the viaduct was completed in 1915, a special stairway near the center provided a route to the island rocks and Cooper's Cave. It permitted visitors to see the hiding place from James Fenimore Cooper's world-famous novel *The Last of the Mohicans*. For many years, the staircase was a major tourist attraction.

Two

THE ECONOMY

COOLIDGE & BENTLEY, C. 1901. The store at 126 Glen Street sold clothing off the rack, but the gentlemen's clothing department featured the services of a merchant tailor. A sign in the doorway advertises pants. The civic-minded owners advertise for a pumpkin pie festival. The pumpkins appear to be mostly green.

THE G. E. HUPMAN TRAVELING STORE, C. 1888. George Hupman was one of the many peddlers in the area at this time. Many of the farms in the outlying areas were far enough away that trips to the village for supplies were limited. Peddlers were able to make a living by selling staples door-to-door. The horses in this image have long coverings made of strings to move about and chase flies away.

VARNEY BROTHERS, C. 1900. The Varney Brothers store, at 27–27½ South Street, sold groceries, flour, feed, hay, and biscuits. Wooden crates were made to hold baskets of strawberries. The street in this photograph is still dirt, but limestone curbing has been added to the sidewalk. In the left doorway is Selleck J. Varney, and in the right doorway is Jacob Varney.

CHARLES A. HOVEY, C. 1890. Charles A. Hovey Sr. ran a fruit, fish, and oysters shop at 129 Glen Street. He carried domestic and foreign fruits. His son was a clerk for Eugene Theobald in his ice and wood business on Maple Street. By 1901, Charles Hovey Jr. and Sr. ran a fruit and ice company at 14½ Maple Street.

DELONG & SON, C. 1870. Zopher Delong came to Glens Falls in 1860, establishing a hardware store on Warren Street with a partner. When he moved the store to Glen Street after the big fire in 1864, he partnered with his son. It was primarily a hardware store but included stoves, fireplaces, and other things needed to develop a home of quality. In this view, lanterns hang in the window of the store.

THE J. L. KENWORTHY STORE, C. 1890. The Kenworthy store was located at 12–14 Warren Street. It started in 1842 with a partnership between Nobel Peck and John Kenworthy and was called N. Peck & Company, making and selling tinware. When Peck died, Kenworthy took over and ran the business. The store's nickname was the Bear Garden because a group of older men would meet there and "growl about something or other." During Kenworthy's ownership, the store sold crockery, glassware, stoves, tinware, silver plate, cutlery, woodenware, house furnishings, and fishing tackle.

THE BRESLAW BROTHERS' FIRST STORE, 1907. Jay and Samuel Breslaw rented a small vacant store at 80 Glen Street, dealing mainly in stoves and ranges. The business moved several times, and the Breslaw Brothers store settled at 234 Glen Street. The store was the first of a chain of what would become 14 stores.

MOYNIHAN & FOLEY, C. 1915. In 1901, at 88 Glen Street (northwest corner of Park and Glen), there was a wine and liquor store called "the Glen," but by 1915, Patrick H. Moynihan and Daniel Foley were the owners. The store sold wines, beers, and liquors and also included a pool and billiards hall. Hard times befell the business in 1918 because of Prohibition, and it closed.

THE O. C. SMITH STORE, C. 1900. O. C. Smith ran a store at the southwest corner of Glen Street in the Crandall Block. The crates pictured here were used to hold smaller baskets of strawberries. Reflections in the windows show homes in the present-day Crandall City Park. A gas lamp hangs over the doorway. Bananas sit on a small table on the sidewalk, and a Hires product is stacked in a window.

I. N. SCOTT & SON, 1895. The store at 18 Ridge Street sold washbasins, chamber pots, and baskets of apples. The man with the bowler is Elroy Weaver, an employee, followed by George Scott, I. N. Scott, and Walter W. Scott. The windows show the reflections of the businesses across the street.

HALL'S ICE CREAM, C. 1915. Hall's Ice Cream, at 4 Maple Street, is pictured here. Next to it is a home, and to the right of that home is the cupola of the Henry Crandall Carriage House. On the left we see Hulda Eldridge. Fourth from the left is Powel Smith, and to the left of the tree is Byron Hall himself. A delivery wagon sits between the store and the house.

THE HALL ICE CREAM COMPANY, C. 1925. After a successful beginning in its modest building at 4 Maple Street, the Hall Ice Cream Company moved into its new facility on the same site. A lighted marquee appears over the door, and a modern truck owned by the company is parked in front.

27

EAGLE CLOTHING, C. 1903. Julius Jacobson founded his business in 1889 at 148 Glen Street across from the YMCA building (visible in the reflection in the window of the store). His wife, Pauline, was the bookkeeper. The store burned in the fire of 1902, and this photograph was taken just after the business reopened. The center two figures are most likely Julius and Pauline. A half-mannequin displays a pair of pants while a jacket hangs on what appears to be a dress form. Racks hold pants that are sold for 25¢. Note the gas lamp over the door and the closed awning above the windows. The family retained ownership of the business until 1945.

THE EAGLE CLOTHING COMPANY SALES FORCE, C. 1892. Personal attention was the rule of the day, and very little clothing was purchased "off the rack." Here, two clerks measure a man and boy for pants and a topcoat. Vests were very much in fashion, as seen on both customers. From left to right are William T. Burt, James Lynch, William Padden, and Henry Moss. All are employees of the store and are obviously posing for an advertising photograph.

THE EAGLE CLOTHING STORE, C. 1920. This interior view of the Eagle store shows a men's section with celluloid collars on a rack on the left. Neckties are in the case on the right. The wooden floors and tin ceiling reflect an earlier time of construction. The man second from the left is Byron Jacobson, and behind the counter in the center is his father, Julius, founder of the store.

THE INTERIOR OF P. P. BRALEY'S STORE, C. 1890. In 1884, Pliney Pierce Braley opened a store that sold books at 133–135 Glen Street. The store also carried porcelain products, crockery, glassware, and wire baskets. The man second from the left is P. P. Braley, and the woman is Ethel Stone. The man at the right is Clayton Crannell. Electric lights hang from the tin ceiling.

GOODSON BROTHERS, 1906.
The Goodson brothers,
William, Isaac, Leonard,
and George, moved their
business from Ridge Street
to a new location at 136–
138 Glen Street in 1906.
It became the Goodson
Brothers store
and featured dry goods.

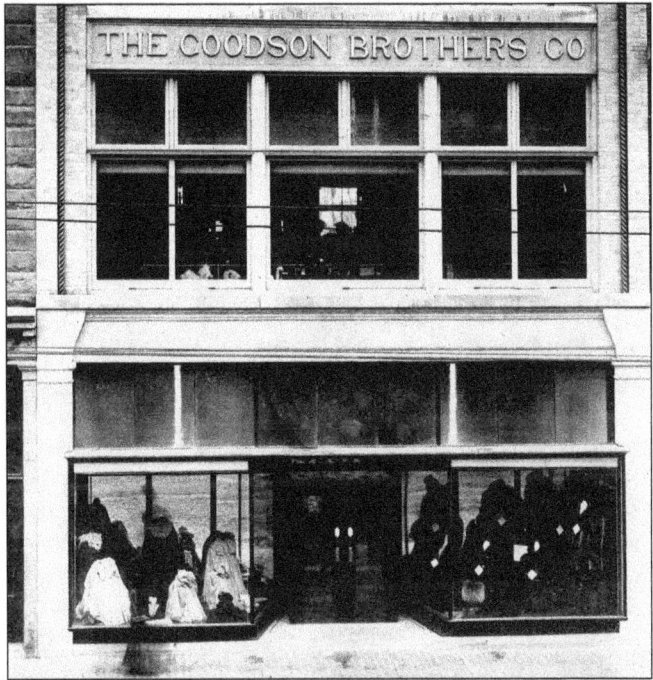

GOODSON BROTHERS, 1906. The third floor of the Goodson Brothers store on Glen Street featured suits, coats, skirts, and furs. Concerts were held in the store every Saturday during its first year of operation.

ERLANGER'S, C. 1924. Erlanger's opened in 1922 at 118 Glen Street. Brothers Julius and Lester Erlanger purchased this building at 126 Glen Street (the southwest corner of Glen and Exchange Streets) in 1923. At first, the upper floors were rented to other businesses, but soon the store expanded into this space.

B. B. FOWLER DRY GOODS, C. 1902. At 130–132 Glen Street, this store was advertised as one of the finest shops between Troy and Montreal. The first shop on this site burned in 1884, and this building opened in 1902, boasting "the embodiment of the highest class of Dry Goods."

32

THE JOSEPH FOWLER SHIRT AND COLLAR COMPANY, C. 1900. This prominent building at 114 Glen Street opened in 1897. The trellises pictured here were on the residential property owned by Dr. Thomas Foulds, previously owned by Jeremiah Finch, whose daughter married Dr. Foulds. The Joseph Fowler Shirt and Collar Company and the Glens Falls Box Company occupied the upstairs of the collar company building.

THE EMPIRE AUTO COMPANY, C. 1915–1920. Prior to 1912, the building was the home of Joubert and White Wagon Makers. In 1913–1914, it became the home of the Empire Automobile Company, selling Chevrolet and Cadillac automobiles. Warren Street was paved with brick and had trolley tracks imbedded in it. The cars pictured here are parked on Jay Street.

THE OLD STONE WAGON SHOP, C. 1880. The building was located between the Hudson River and the Feeder Canal on the east side of Glen Street. It was sometimes referred to as the Old Stone Store and was allegedly home of Civil War general Daniel Sickles. The Methodist church in Glens Falls may have started in this building also.

THE BLACKSMITH SHOP, C. 1900. Julien Beaudet ran a successful blacksmith shop on Park Street after moving from a shop on the Glen Street hill. Advertising himself as a "scientific horseshoer," Beaudet was famous for dealing with trotters and pacers at the racetrack in Glens Falls. Beaudet is fourth from left in the photograph. (Beaudet photograph.)

THE GLENS FALLS INSURANCE COMPANY, C. 1880. The company had its meager beginnings in two different offices in Glen Street buildings. When more space was needed in 1859, a building designed by Hiram Krum was built on Glen Street. Krum designed the building as a home so it might have resale value if the business failed. It was located in the block that now contains Crandall City Park.

THE SECOND GLENS FALLS INSURANCE COMPANY, C. 1891. The second home of the company on Glen Street was completed in 1891. In this photograph, workmen manually place curbs along the dirt street, and elm trees partially obscure the Church of the Messiah. The iron fence encircles the 20-year-old Civil War Monument.

MOVING THE GLENS FALLS INSURANCE COMPANY, C. 1911–1912. Without the use of modern conveniences, the building was moved across Glen Street to become the Masonic Temple. To the left of the building is the Church of the Messiah, and to the right are the businesses on the east side of Bay Street. As with any engineering feat, an audience is attracted to the work.

THE GLENS FALLS INSURANCE COMPANY, 1912–1913. The Glens Falls Insurance Company outgrew its facility on the corner of Glen and Bay Streets. The building moved across Glen Street to become the Masonic Temple, and construction for a new one began on the old site. (Bayle photograph.)

THE GLENS FALLS INSURANCE COMPANY, 1912. Considerable progress was made between November and December 1912. (Bayle photograph.)

THE GLENS FALLS INSURANCE COMPANY, 1913. The facility was completed in 1913 and quickly became a fixture in the community. (Bayle photograph.)

THE ROCKWELL HOUSE, C. 1900. Located on Glen Street at Bank Square, the hotel opened on February 22, 1872, with accommodations for 150 guests. The hotel had spacious grounds and offered amenities for "home-like comfort and quiet elegance," with many upscale shops. In the 1920s, the front porch was removed and the name changed to Hotel Rockwell.

THE CITY HOTEL, 1899. The City Hotel was located at 9 Warren Street in 1899, although Glens Falls was at that time still a village. By 1902, the name was changed to the Grand Hotel, then to the Arnet. By 1908, it was called the New City Hotel, and in 1910 it was known as the Warren Inn.

THE AMERICAN HOUSE, C. THE 1870S. A hotel was constructed of wood on the northwest corner of Glen and South Streets; its large porch entrance faced south. The Glens Falls–Lake George stagecoach stopped here. The barns were used for the horses and coaches of hotel guests. Fire destroyed the hotel on August 5, 1879.

THE AMERICAN HOUSE, C. THE MID-1880S. George Pardo, manager, built a brick version of the American House in late 1879 and early 1880. The three-story structure's porch was relocated to Glen Street. Although trolley tracks are evident in the street, horses still pulled carriages along South Street. Private residences prevailed to the north of the hotel.

HOTEL RULIFF, 1899. During the 1899 construction of the Empire Theater on South Street, the American Hotel was renamed Hotel Ruliff. The hotel served the lower Adirondack tourist trade in addition to renting rooms for entertainers from the Empire Theater. It also provided space for celebrations sponsored by the theater.

THE GLOBE HOTEL BAR, C. 1910. This hotel, although it went through several names and owners, was by 1897 known as the Globe. The inside of the Globe Hotel reflected the period with its spittoons, brass rails, and highly polished bar. In 1898, Theodore Roosevelt was to make a speech in the Glens Falls Opera House, but because of the extremely large crowd, the event was moved to the outside steps of the Globe Hotel.

THE ARGENT, C. 1900. Merritt Ames, local silver refiner, built an apartment house at 17–19 Sherman Avenue, next to his home and business, for investment purposes. He named it L'Argent, the French word for silver.

TELEPHONE OPERATORS, 1917. Telephone service arrived in Glens Falls in 1879. One day and one night operator served 55 phones from the Colvin Building. Eventually there were two competing companies—the Hudson River Telephone Company and the Commercial Union Telephone Company. Having two phones in a home was required, as the equipment of the two companies was not compatible. By 1917, many independent phone companies merged, making life easier.

THE BEMIS EYE SANITARIUM, C. 1890. The sanitarium specialized in treating eye disorders. Dr. Edward H. Bemis used his patented magnetic vaporizer, a machine that apparently caused hemorrhaging in the eye, thereby creating a cleansing action. By 1896, more than 58,000 such treatments were given. Guests stayed in the apartments on Sherman Avenue, now called Sherman Square.

THE BEMIS COMPLEX, C. 1890. Whole families accompanied the patient and stayed an average of six weeks during the treatment. They stayed in apartments such as the Marion House on East Notre Dame Street near the Allen House on Glen. The Marion House was named after Dr. Bemis's wife. Fresh fruits, vegetable, and meat were grown on the Bemis farm in Wilton each summer to feed the numerous visitors.

THE BEMIS HOME, C. 1872. This stately home on the corner of Glen and Sherman belongs to Dr. E. H. Bemis. It was referred to as the Sherman House, after Augustus Sherman, and is now the home of the Glens Falls Senior Citizen Center.

THE ALLEN HOUSE, C. 1872. Dr. Edward Bemis ran an eye clinic complex that included the Allen House at the corner of Glen and Union Streets. It was the main treatment center for the clinic. Patients from all over the United States, and some from Europe, arrived regularly to stay at boardinghouses on Union Street and the one visible here on East Notre Dame.

THE WEAVER BROTHERS' BARBERSHOP, C. 1910. This shop was located at the southwest corner of Glen and Exchange Streets. Five barbers were needed to take care of customers, as men often went to a barber regularly for a shave. The brothers Jay L. and Algie J. Weaver shared the building with four other businesses. The building exists today as a brewpub.

GLEN STREET, C. 1905. In this photograph, the Greek American Fruit Company displays its goods on the sidewalk. Large bunches of bananas hang out for selection. A cigar store Indian advertises domestic "segars." Bicycles and carts are visible, as is a shoeshine stand on the left. Awnings kept out the direct rays of the sun during the time before air conditioning.

THE PEYSER FACTORY, 1898. The Peyser and Morrison Shirt Company was located at 211–217 Warren Street. In 1916, it became H. & F. Binch Company, which manufactured lace. By 1971, it operated as Native Lace and Textiles. It is currently run as Native Textiles. Ephraim Potter, local architect, received an award for the design of the building.

THE PAPER BOX COMPANY, 1905. John Leggett came from Troy, New York, c. 1902 and began the Glens Falls Paper Box Manufacturing Company at 230 Maple Street. The building has been remodeled and is now the home of the Warren and Washington County Association for Mental Health.

45

THE CLARK GLOVE FACTORY, C. THE LATE 1920S. The factory, built *c.* 1922, produced fine ladies' gloves. Gloves were an important part of a cultured lady's attire. The location was formerly the home of Mrs. Samuel Pruyn.

THE YORKE SHIRT COMPANY, C. 1915. In this photograph, shirts are displayed in the company store on the corner of Pine and West (Broad) Streets. The sign advertises over 21,600 shirts made from 68,400 yards of material in a week. This is only one of many shirt factories that existed in Glens Falls over the years.

A MOVING SALE, C. 1915. The Rugg & Moren store, at the corner of Warren and Glen Streets, moved from this site to the YMCA building at 147 Glen Street. The clothier, hatter, and outfitter advertised "cash and one price to all." The trolley tracks, wires, and car pictured here indicate a busy intersection.

THE GLENS FALLS LIME KILNS, C. 1875. The lime industry was the second most important industry after lumbering in Glens Falls. Extremely pure limestone deposits, together with a wood-burning process of preparation, produced the finest quality lime used in the manufacturing of cement. The finished lime was shipped out of the area in wooden barrels, keeping coopers very busy.

47

GATHERING FUEL, 1897. Here, immigrant women gather scrap fuels near the Jointa Lime Company kilns. Hard times for newcomers make gathering fuel a necessity.

Three

STREET SCENES

AN AERIAL VIEW OF GLENS FALLS, C. 1890. The chimney of the Glens Falls Electric Company provided a place for a photograph of the village. Visible in this image is the fountain of Fountain Square. The tower on Ridge Street in the center of the picture is on the firehouse. The large slanted roof in the right of the photograph belongs to the Glens Falls Opera House on Warren Street.

THE CORNER OF RIDGE AND GLEN STREET, C. 1890. Daniel Peck's grocery was at the left side of the Ridge Street intersection. Next-door was a store selling flour, grain, hay, and feed. The building on the right corner of Ridge Street was the site of the original Wing's Tavern. Wagons, awnings, and the fountain give a clear picture of downtown life.

LAYING THE TRACKS, C. 1891. Electric trolleys arrived in Glens Falls. Tracks had to be laid by hand in the brick streets. Horses and wagons delivered supplies. Here, an audience gathers to observe the work.

DECORATION DAY, MAY 30, 1872. In 1866, voters approved $8,000 to construct a monument to honor area soldiers killed in the Civil War. Because the monument actually cost $12,000 to complete, R. T. Baxter, the builder, had to absorb the cost since his contract was for the lower figure. At the dedication in 1872, people dressed in their finest. The circular iron fence surrounding the monument no longer exists.

GLEN STREET, C. 1890. The elm trees form a canopy over Glen Street even in winter. The white building pictured here is the first building constructed for the Glens Falls Insurance Company. The building was designed as a house so that it would have resale value if the company failed. These buildings were located in what is today Crandall City Park. According to Henry Crandall's wishes, the park was supposed to be called Crandall Place.

LOOKING SOUTH ON GLEN STREET, C. 1890. This dirt street had horse posts to tie up animals in this busy commercial area. Horse-drawn wagons drove through the street. The pillars on the right are on the front of a bank. The area on the left is now the site of a fast-food restaurant and the Glens Falls Civic Center.

GLEN STREET, C. 1880. The American Hotel was at the corner of South and Glen Streets. In this view looking north, the trees nearly cover the street. The horse-drawn carriage was the main form of transportation at the time. The dirt street had limestone curbing and a coach step. A gas lamp by the hotel lit the street at night.

GLEN STREET, C. 1910. Eagle Clothing is on the right in this image, with the street going south to the Rockwell House at the left, just out of view. A bicycle is parked at the Colvin Building (which exists today), home of the first telephone office. Just past the clock is the B. B. Fowler building, which also still exists.

GLEN STREET GARDENS, C. 1895. The landscape of Glens Falls included residences among the businesses on Glen Street. Jeremiah Finch had a home in the middle of the village opposite the First National Bank and the YMCA building. He maintained large gardens on his property. Residences are still maintained to the left of the bank in the area that became City Park.

SHERMAN AVENUE GARDENS, 1922. Gardens between Sherman Avenue and West Notre Dame Street stretched behind 61–65 Sherman Avenue. Middle-class families commonly grew crops. The gardens pictured here were located behind houses that still exist on West Notre Dame. Children spent time tending corn, cabbage, beans, and some vine crops.

RESULTS OF A FIRE, 1864. Because of the area's proximity to the low-cost lumber in the Adirondacks, most buildings here were constructed of wood. In 1864, a fire started in the kitchen of a downtown hotel and then spread quickly from street to street until more than 100 buildings were consumed. Shelters were set up among the ruins, and the city quickly began the rebuilding process.

AFTER THE FIRE, 1864. Business resumed as soon as temporary buildings were set up. Staple's Glen's Falls Market was one of the first to reopen.

THE VILLAGE HALL AND TWO FIRE DEPARTMENTS, C. 1900. The village hall was completed in 1900. Available space in the extra rooms was rented to businesses. When the village was incorporated as a city in 1908, village hall became city hall. The two-division fire department was located in a converted barn, with the Lapham Hose Company No. 3 on the left and the M. B. Little Hose Company No. 2 on the right.

CRANDALL CITY PARK, 1924. By 1924, all the residences in Crandall City Park were gone. Large elm trees lined the street with hedgelike borders at the sidewalks. The park benches pictured here are arranged along the inner sidewalk, and the "new" insurance company building appears in the distance.

THE RED LINE FRUIT COMPANY, C. 1911–1912. Martin J. Callahan owned the business at 7 West Street, now Broad Street. Delivery wagons, an early car, fancy grillwork on the balcony, and wooden barrels were common during this era.

WINTER ON SOUTH STREET, C. 1900. South Street ran east toward Glen Street. The South-End Livery was where visitors attending the Empire Theater kept their horses. Performers at the Empire could stay at the Empire Hotel (left) or at the Madden Hotel, with its white balconies (right). The snowbanks form a background for two boys wearing knickers and knee socks.

THE INTERSECTION OF RIDGE, WARREN, AND GLEN STREETS, C. 1900. Trolleys arrived in Glens Falls by 1891, but most private transportation relied on horses. Notice the overhead wires for electric trolleys. Sleighs needed streets to be cleared of deep snow, leaving a packed surface

so the runners could travel efficiently. Horses and wagons were used to clear the intersection of deeper snow, and large rollers packed down the remainder. A gas street lamp is visible in front of the Rugg & Moren store.

THE GLENS FALLS OPERA HOUSE, C. 1890. The Glens Falls Opera House opened on Warren Street in November 1871. It provided a venue not only for opera but also for concerts, plays, lectures, and walking and bicycle races. It burned in the fire of 1884 but was quickly rebuilt. It became the Rialto Theater in 1918. Warren Street was unpaved but had cement sidewalks.

LOOKING WEST ON WARREN STREET, C. 1890. Warren Street was unpaved but had limestone curbing. The spire pictured here was on St. Mary's Roman Catholic Church. This was a residential area with fences and horse posts up and down the street. The Rockwell House is at the far end where Glen Street intersects.

WARREN STREET, C. 1880. A firemen's exhibition drew crowds on Warren Street. Men wearing traditional hats and suits made up most of the crowd. Spectators enjoyed the activities from rooftops. The first spire on the right is on the Presbyterian church, and the farther spire is on St. Mary's Roman Catholic Church. The spire on the left is on the Methodist church.

FOUNTAIN SQUARE WITH A WAGON, C. THE LATE 1800S. Transportation progress is evident when a horse-driven coach, trolley wires, and tracks appear in the same picture. There are awnings on the buildings, and a pool hall and cigar store can be seen on Glen Street. As one looks up Ridge Street, the city's famous elm trees are recognizable. The dress worn by the woman crossing the street reflects the style of the period.

THE CRANDALL BLOCK, C. 1885. Corey's Store (with the horseshoe-shaped sign), P. H. Millinery and Dress Goods, the O. C. Smith store, and a box factory were among the businesses located in this commercial complex c. 1874. By 1962, the building at the corner of Glen and South Streets was mostly empty and was sold to a local bank. It was destroyed by fire on May 27, 1963.

GLEN STREET, 1925. Policeman Frank Lyons crosses the trolley tracks on brick-lined Glen Street on the day of the Rialto fire on Warren Street. A Saratoga pumper is parked around the corner from it in front of the Peabody Hotel on Glen.

WARREN STREET, 1900. The home of Martha Mahala Rugge was at 40 Warren Street. In this photograph, the trolley runs down the middle of the street, but horse posts still exist on the south side of the road. The stately elm trees are ubiquitous here, as throughout the village.

THE GLENS FALLS ARMORY, C. 1905. The armory, at 147 Warren Street, was built in 1895. Company K was here for more than 80 years. The building currently houses units of the New York National Guard. The Hyde Museum complex is now located on the wide expanse of land.

Four

RESIDENCES

THE CRANDALL HOME, 1905. The home of lumberman and philanthropist Henry Crandall was located on Glen Street, now part of Crandall City Park. He also established Crandall Park on Upper Glen Street. He donated his home and provided money to create and support a public library.

THE ZOPHER DELONG HOME, C. 1920. Zopher DeLong bought a small farmhouse at 220 Glen Street in 1860. Between 1867 and 1869, an addition was put on. The family owned a hardware store, and many supplies could be obtained at cost. The home remained in the family until 1966, when Juliet Chapman donated the home to the Glens Falls–Queensbury Historical Association. It is now the home of the Chapman Historical Museum.

THE THEODORE DELONG HOME, C. 1901. Theodore DeLong, one of the sons of Zopher and Catherine, resided at 216 Glen Street. This Greek Revival home has the traditional triangular pediment at the roofline. A wraparound porch is seen here rather than the pillars found on DeLong's brother's home (seen on page 90).

THE SISSON HOUSE, C. 1880. The second frame house in the village was built by Abraham Wing's younger brother, Edward, right after the Revolutionary War. It was located at the point where Glen and Bay Streets intersect. Four others owned the house before James Sisson purchased it in 1834. Sisson married the granddaughter of Edward Wing, who lived in the house as a child. After the Civil War, Sisson sold the point of his property to the town of Queensbury for $1,000 for the erection of the Civil War Monument. When Sisson died in 1879, Mr. Spiers bought the house. It was torn down in 1890, when the Glens Falls Insurance Company bought the property.

THE FINCH HOME, C. 1900. Jeremiah W. Finch owned one of the last residential properties in the center of the business district on Glens Street. His home, with its elegant fenced-in gardens, was just south of the Crandall Block, where the Glens Falls National Bank is today.

THE COOLIDGE HOME, C. 1890. The house at 161 Glen Street was the residence of Jonathan Coolidge, a Glens Falls merchant and onetime president of the Tancolla Company. He was also president of the Glens Falls Terra Cotta and Brick Company. The home was located in what is now Crandall City Park.

THE BADIALI HOME, C. 1925. Julien Z. Badiali, consulting engineer, lived at 240 Glen Street on the southwest corner of Notre Dame Street. The side porches and tower are architecturally unique. The home was located on the site of the present-day Presbyterian church.

THE KING HOME, C. 1913. This stately home at 304 Glen Street belonged to Charles F. King, a lawyer. He was a partner in the firm of Potter, Kellogg and King, first at 3 Park Street and then at 144 Glen Street. The elegant second-story porch adds a unique look to the home.

THE SPIERS HOME, C. 1890. William Spiers's home was at 213 Glen Street, next to the Church of the Messiah. He was a successful businessman in the lumber and paper industries and in horse breeding. He was able to bail out Eugene Ashley's financially strapped project to build a dam in the Hudson River. He earned the right to have the dam named after him: Spiers Falls Dam.

THE MOYNEHAN HOME, C. 1910. The Patrick Moynehan home was at the corner of Glen Street and what is now Washington Street. He worked his way up in the lumber business, finally becoming owner. He moved to Glens Falls in 1890 and became the largest real estate owner in the village. He erected the Moynehan Building at the corner of Ridge and Glen Streets, now home to Scoville Jewelers.

THE FOWLER HOME, 1910. Byron B. Fowler was the founder of the B. B. Fowler Company, a dry goods store at 130–132 Glen Street. In this photograph, his home at 324 (now 542) Glen Street is surrounded by huge snowbanks that must be removed. The remainder must be packed down so sleighs can travel smoothly over the streets.

THE COLVIN HOME, C. 1885. The Honorable Addison B. Colvin lived on the southeast corner of Glen and Chester Streets. He built the Colvin Building on Glen Street on the site of his family home. Colvin was founder of the *Glens Falls Times*, the Glens Falls Trust Company (with the Colvin Clock in front), and the Empire Theater. He was the New York State treasurer from 1893 and 1898.

THE MCGREGOR HOME, C. 1880. Duncan McGregor bought his home, built by Capt. Sidney Berry, at the top of Glen Street hill. The stone retaining wall is still in existence, but the home was replaced with J. E. Sawyer and Company. McGregor owned many acres of land, including a mountain named after him in Wilton.

THE PARKS' GARDENS, C. 1905. The gardens at the home of Frederick Parks show the elegance of the mansions in town at the time. The side of the home faced south, and the front faced Glen Street. Frederick Parks was the district manager of International Paper Company. He lived at 219 Glen Street for many years in the general area of what is now the Continental Insurance Company.

THE HALSEY WING HOME, PRE-1870. Here, Harriet and Halsey Wing sit on the porch of their Jay Street home. Halsey Wing, great-grandson of Abraham Wing, was a wealthy lawyer and was in the lime business with John Keenan. Harriet Wing organized the Ladies Patriotic Association during the Civil War. They lived in this home until after the Civil War.

THE WING HOUSE, C. 1870. Built of Philadelphia brick in the late 1860s by Hiram Krum, the Halsey Wing mansion was located on Warren Street. The grounds covered about three acres sloping down toward the river. The property was located between what is now the armory and Oakland Avenue and is the site of the Hyde Museum complex.

THE COOL HOME, C. 1900. Keyes Cool was the first mayor of the city of Glens Falls, in 1908. His home was located at 50 Warren Street. Arriving in Glens Falls from Vermont in 1828, he and his brother helped erect the first Methodist church, on Church Street. He became involved in the lime business, opening an office at the foot of Fredella Street, which he passed on to his sons.

THE ORDWAY HOME, C. 1895. Jones Ordway was a lumber baron who owned thousands of acres of wood lots in the Adirondacks. His home was at 142 Warren Street in Glens Falls. He donated $50,000 toward the YMCA building on Glen Street. Whether by accident or deliberately, his name is misspelled on his monument, the largest in the Glens Falls Cemetery.

THE ROSEKRANS HOME, C. 1890. Judge Enoch Rosekrans built his home at 62 Warren Street c. 1850. It was converted to a hospital run by Dr. Lemon Thompson. Later, Eugene Ashley owned it, but it eventually became the rectory of St. Mary's. The building in the background is the Methodist church, which was demolished to make room for St. Mary's Academy.

THE KRUM HOME, C. 1880. The home of Hiram Krum at 133 Warren Street was built c. 1865. Like many of the homes built in the 1860s, it is Second Empire, Italianate with a mansard roof. Krum is the village's leading contractor and builder. He was responsible for building the first Glens Falls Insurance Company, the Rockwell House, the First American Hotel, and the Warren Street Presbyterian Church.

THE CARRIAGE HOUSE, C. 1901. The beautiful garden and carriage house pictured here were part of the property of George R. Finch at the corner of Warren and Prospect Streets. The size of the building with its gambrel roof clearly indicates wealth. Finch is a banker, lumberman, and Democratic Party leader. The property is now the site of the Eden Park Nursing Home.

THE LITTLE GARDENS, 1898. Meredith Little, who worked in a local insurance company with M. Loomis, lived at 84 Warren Street. He has elegant formal gardens, a fountain, and a greenhouse behind his home.

A WARREN STREET HOME, C. 1900. The original home on this site was owned by Abraham Wing. It was purchased c. 1823 by William McDonald, added to, and remodeled. The house was removed to make way for the Glens Falls Home for Women in 1903, funded by William McEchron.

THE GOODMAN HOME, C. 1920. Samuel Goodman lived on Park Street. The home was built near a ravine that runs down the hill toward Mohican Street. It became the Sullivan and Minahan Funeral Home but is now a parking lot.

ALONZO MORGAN, C. 1885. Alonzo Morgan started out in the saddle- and harness-making business. He later entered into land developing. He owned land from the top of the Glen Street hill and opened up Park and Elm Streets all the way to South Street. He owned 42½ acres with Sheldon Benedict on the north side of Warren Street and opened up Maple Street and many side streets.

THE MORGAN HOME, C. 1885. Alonzo Morgan built a Greek Revival home at 130 Maple Street in 1840. A gas lamp sits near the gate to the yard. After the death of his wife in 1873, he sold everything and retired to a farm.

THE LAPHAM HOUSE, C. 1910. From 1816 to 1840, the Warren County High School existed on Ridge Street in what is now Crandall City Park. When the principal, Obadiah Alma, died in 1840, the school closed and the building was converted into a private dwelling. Mr. Lapham was in the railroad and lumber business and served on the board of education for the local school district. He was the board president for a period of time. On the porch here are Grandma Lapham and Aunt Nancy. Helen Lapham Lewis is on the steps, while Margaret and Nell Lewis are on the lawn.

THE CARRIAGE HOUSE, C. 1910. Jerome Lapham's carriage house and barns were located behind his Ridge Street home. The elegant trim work and cupola add to the otherwise functional building. The building was later converted into Honigsbaum's Fashion Store, and more recently into the home of Lower Adirondack Regional Arts Center (LARAC).

THE LAPHAM FAMILY, C. 1890. The Lapham family dates back to before 1800 in this area. Here, the family poses for a picture in their home at 50 Ridge Street.

THE LAPHAM HOUSE, 1890. Mortimer Lapham had a home and a wagon-making business at 38 Ridge Street. Ten years later, Benjamin Lapham sold and repaired pumps at this address. The tower in the background was from the first Ridge Street Fire Station. The site of the home is now the location of the Glens Falls City Hall.

THE DIX HOME, C. 1890. The James Lawton Dix home, on Ridge Street, was built c. 1850. The property ran between Lawton and Dix Avenues. The streets are obviously named after James Lawton Dix. Dix owned a foundry at the corner of Glen and Canal (Oakland) Streets. His son John was born in the house on Christmas Day 1860 and became governor of New York State in 1910.

THE McEchron Home, c. 1900. William McEchron was a lumber baron who gave generously to many worthy causes. The McEchron home on Ridge Street was given to the city in 1920 to be used as a health center. The house to the right was the home and office of Dr. George Little. The fountain was on the Lapham property that is now part of Crandall City Park.

THE Gayger Home, Pre-1898. The corner of Maple and Ridge Streets was the location of the William H. Gayger home. Located at 60 Ridge Street, the home was next-door to the Jerome Lapham House, in the corner that is now Crandall City Park. William Gayger is pictured on the left, and his boarder, Robert C. Carter, a clerk for the Glens Falls Insurance Company, is on the right.

THE FOULDS MANSION, C. 1910. Dr. and Mrs. Thomas Foulds took a yearlong worldwide honeymoon in 1900 while their grand mansion at 97 Ridge Street was being built. Mrs. Foulds was the daughter of famed lumberman Jeremiah Finch. Frank Hoffman purchased the home with plans to build a nursing home, but the home was torn down during urban renewal and is now the site of the Ahlstrom Complex.

AN INTERIOR VIEW OF THE FOULDS MANSION, C. 1910. Parquet floors and stately arches graced the parlor of the Thomas Foulds home on Ridge Street. The entryway featured magnificent columns and a grand staircase. A huge fireplace was located in the library. The rooms were equipped with electricity.

83

THE BIRDSALL HOME, C. 1885. Dr. Stephen Birdsall came to Glens Falls in 1884 and lived in the home at 142 Ridge Street. His son Edgar drove the horse and buggy for his father's house calls. After medical school, Edgar, a pioneer radiologist for northeastern New York, brought x-ray equipment into the area from Germany. He was chief radiologist at the Glens Falls Hospital from 1922 until 1959.

THE BIRDSALL FAMILY, 1885. The family of Dr. Stephen Birdsall is pictured on the porch of their Ridge Street home. From left to right are Stephen, daughter Mabel, wife Josephine, daughter Agnes, and son Edgar. The home is now an apartment building.

THE CUNNINGHAM HOME, 1910. Col. John Cunningham, Civil War recruiter, resided at 14 Berry Street in 1910. His elegant carriage house appears to the right of the home. He was president of the Glens Falls Insurance Company at the time. He later moved to 90 Ridge Street. Berry Street, unpaved at the time, is now the entrance to the Glens Falls Civic Center.

THE CUNNINGHAM HOME, C. 1919. The home at 90 Ridge Street at the corner of May, was known as the Cunningham house, named after Col. John L. Cunningham. It was first occupied by J. Irving Fowler of the Joseph Fowler Shirt and Collar Company in 1909. Cunningham moved in 1919. The Ridge Street School is visible to the right. The site is now a parking lot for a chain drugstore.

THE CHILDREN OF MARTHA MAKAYLA SHERMAN RUGGE, 1886. The front steps of the Loomis-Dix home at 77 Ridge Street are the setting for this photograph of Martha Rugge's children. From left to right are the following: (front row) Alice, Lulu, Harriet, Helen, and Abbie; (back row) Elizabeth, Catherine, Augustus, and Mary. The home was torn down in the 1960s.

THE SMITH HOME, C. 1900. Orville C. Smith lived at 122 Bay Street with his family. The building still exists today. He owns a wholesale and retail grocery store in the Crandall Block on the southwest corner of South and Glen Streets.

THE EDDY HOME, C. 1890. Dr. Jerome Eddy, physician and surgeon, had an office and home at 13 South Street. The entrance to the office was on the left side of the building. He practiced here until 1915. A gas street lamp is visible by the sidewalk in front of the building. The site is now the parking lot and farmers' market on South Street.

THE CHAPMAN HOME, C. 1910. Dr. George Chapman had his home and office at 23 Elm Street. He was in practice from 1900 until the 1940s. This home stood where the Elm Street parking lot is now.

A STODDARD PORTRAIT, C. 1910. In this photograph, Seneca Ray Stoddard sits at his desk surrounded by the many projects with which he is involved. Best known for his photography, he was also an outstanding cartographer and publisher of Adirondacks guidebooks and maps that are still in use today. He also invented photographic equipment.

THE DINING ROOM, C. 1910. The inside of the Stoddard home was typical for the time. Here, a gas lamp hangs over the table, and an open hutch shows off the family dishes. The room is small but is full of furniture and family things.

THE STODDARD HOME, C. 1910. Pictured here is the backyard of Seneca Ray Stoddard's 22 Elm Street home in Glens Falls. Although his home appears to be in the country, it is well within the limits of the village.

THE WENDALL HOME, C. 1900. First a bookkeeper and then the manager of Freeman's Lumber Company at Feeder Dam, John L. Wendall lived at 5 Cross Street (Clinton Street). The size of the home indicates he belonged to the upper middle class.

THE CUTLER DELONG HOME, C. 1900. Cutler DeLong, one of the sons of Zopher and Catherine, resided at 30 Bay Street. The Greek Revival home featured four pillars and floor-length windows on the first floor. Cutler was the treasurer of the Glens Falls Insurance Company. The Bay Street location is where the insurance company parking lot now exists.

THE REILLY HOME, 1888. George and Phoebe Reilly lived at 16 Gage Avenue at the time of the 1888 blizzard. They obviously dressed for the weather and ventured outside when the storm was over. On the left is Mary T. Reilly, next to Phoebe Reilly. On the far right is George Reilly.

90

Five

Schools and Churches

THE QUAKER MEETINGHOUSE, 1878. Members of the Quaker sect led by Abraham Wing settled in Glens Falls. A meetinghouse and school were established on Bay Road in 1786 and were replaced with a larger frame building on Ridge Road. By 1875, a third building opened on Ridge Street between Fulton and Grand Streets. Worshipers were expected to bring their own personal containers of hot coals for heat.

THE CATHOLIC CHURCH, C. 1880. St. Mary's was established in 1849, when the Diocese of Albany purchased the Methodist church on the corner of Church and Warren Streets. Construction of the new edifice was completed in 1869. Picket fences indicated property lines existing on Warren Street. The top of the steeple was removed after being deemed unsafe.

THE CHURCH OF THE MESSIAH, C. 1885. The church began in a private home in 1840 and soon moved to 83 Ridge Street. The first service in the stone edifice at 202 Glen Street was held on Christmas 1865, with consecration in June 1866. The first church officers included William McDonald, Abraham Wing, Keys Cool, Walter Geer, and Orange Ferris, famous men in Glens Falls history.

THE BAPTIST CHURCH, C. 1887. Baptists began a church in a building on Maple Street in 1840. The present building was completed in 1885 on the same site. Baptists have worshiped on the same site longer than any other denomination in Glens Falls. Private residences are seen to the right of the church.

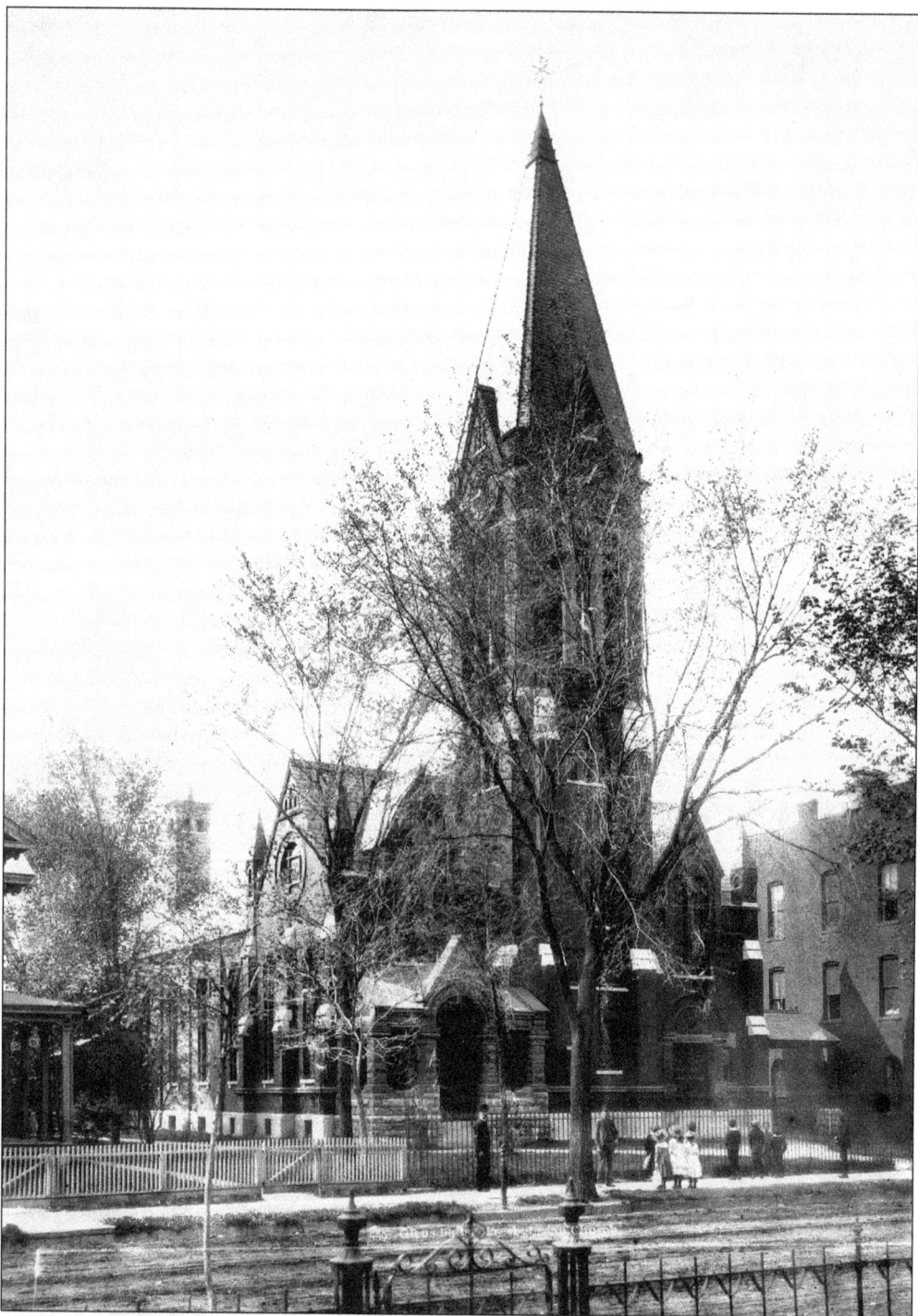

THE PRESBYTERIAN CHURCH, C. 1900. The fourth building of the Presbyterian church, at 23–25 Warren Street, was completed in 1886 after the disastrous fire of 1884. The church was used until 1925, when it was sold to Fred W. Mausert and converted into the State Theater.

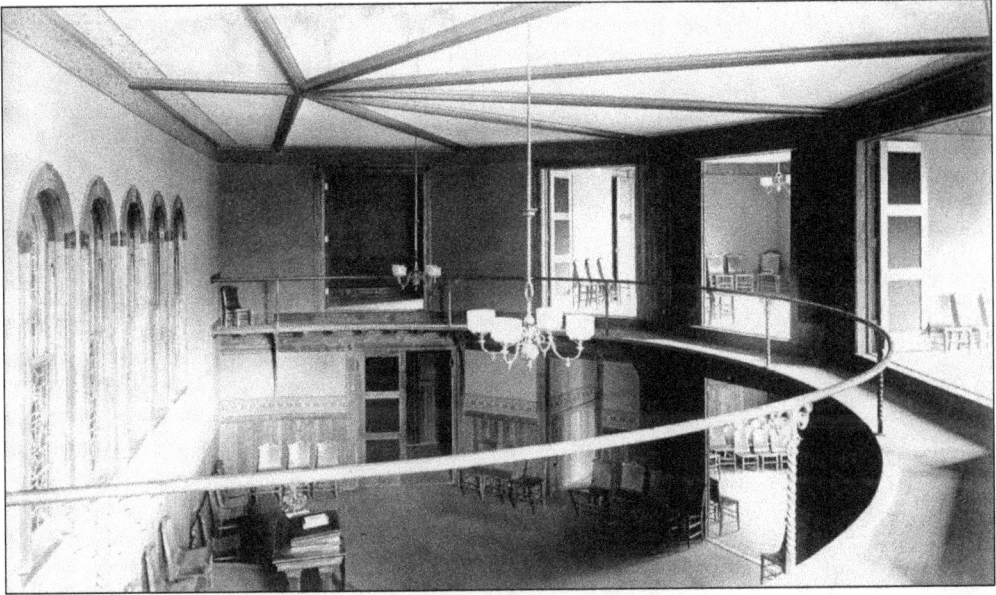

THE PRESBYTERIAN CHAPEL, C. 1900. This spacious gallery in the Presbyterian church, with its downstairs chapel, provided rooms for meetings and other gatherings.

THE MISSION CHURCH, C. 1900. The Mission Church, a Union Society, was located at 82 West (Broad) Street as a satellite of the Presbyterian church. Mission Street was built facing the church.

THE METHODIST CHURCH, C. 1890. In 1865, the third Methodist church opened on the corner of Warren and Church Streets. By the last half of the 1800s, this church was the largest and richest in Glens Falls. The building was sold to St. Mary's in 1905, and the new Methodist church opened in 1907 at Bay and Washington Streets.

THE BIBLE SCHOOL, 1915. For one year, a Bible school was run in a small building on Pruyn's Island. Photographer O. A. Brower was the superintendent of the Methodist Episcopal "Pruyn's Island Chapel."

SEMINARY HILL SCHOOL, C. 1870. Sidney Berry opened a ladies seminary at the corner of Church and Berry Streets in 1836. Run as a finishing school for young ladies, it existed for five years until the academy took over the building while the new Warren Street School was being built. District 19 purchased it in 1842, and it later became the property of St. Mary's.

GLENS FALLS ACADEMY, C. 1880. The school opened in 1841 as a private school for boys, but soon a department for girls was added "in the basement." For many years, it was the only secondary school in Glens Falls, as only 4 percent of the population received a high school education. Three female academy graduates were the first to be awarded New York State Regents diplomas, in 1880.

UNION SCHOOL NO. 2, C. 1892. The South Street School, at the corner of South and West (Broad) Streets, opened in 1891. Under the leadership of Sherman Williams, a concerted effort was made to bring quality education to the general population.

UNION SCHOOL NO. 3, C. 1898. Commonly called the Ridge Street School, this building opened in 1897. Together with Union School Nos. 1 and 2, the Glens Falls School District was complete. Teacher training and a regular high school program were established. The three buildings served the community for nearly 30 years.

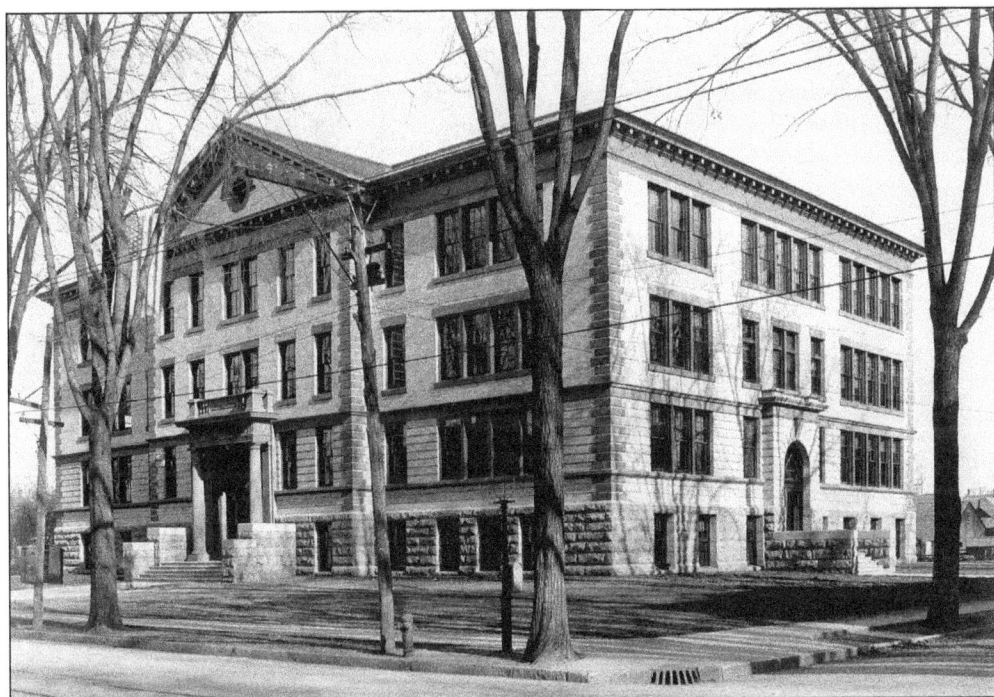

GLENS FALLS HIGH SCHOOL, C. 1906. The Glens Falls High School on Glen Street opened in September 1906. The building replaced the original Union School No. 1, which burned down on December 17, 1902. During the interim, classes were held on the third floor of village hall.

A CLASS PICTURE, 1886. Twenty students appear in this picture at the old Glens Falls High School. Sherman Williams, first superintendent of the consolidated school district, is in the center. The young man in the back row, fourth from the right, is Charles "Bert" Stoddard, son of famed photographer Seneca Ray Stoddard. The girl in the back row, second from the right, is Mary DeLong, granddaughter of Zopher DeLong.

A CHEMISTRY CLASS, 1898. Unidentified students are shown in a high school chemistry class in Union School No. 1. A gas lamp hangs over the table. Girls wear long dresses, and boys wear suits and ties. Two of the students wear lab aprons.

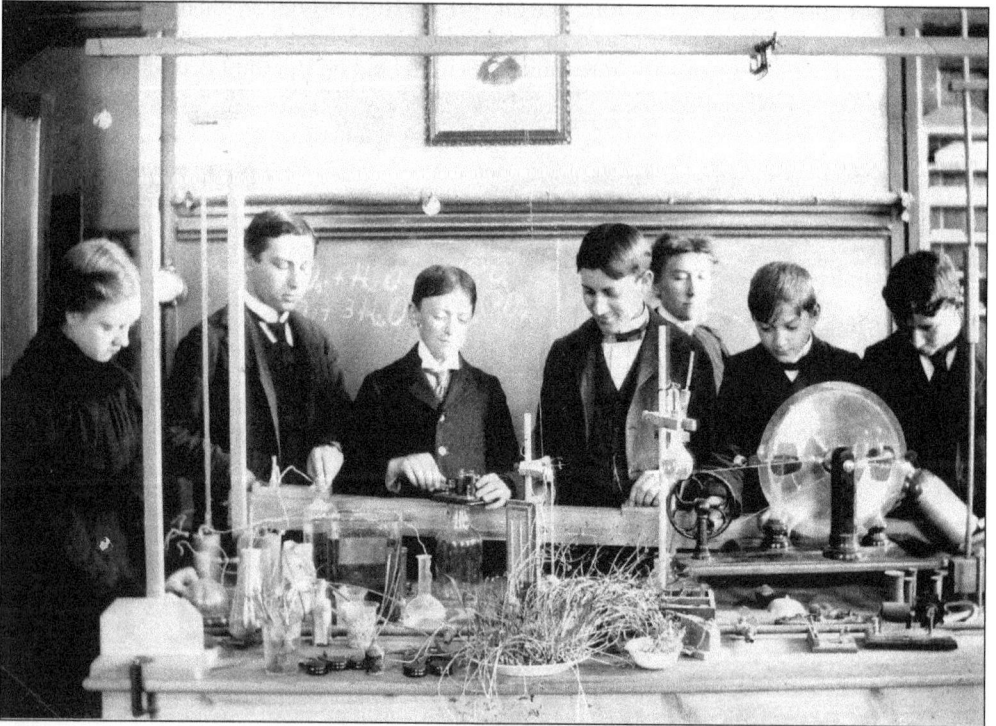

A PHYSICS CLASS, 1897–1898. Here, a physics class at the Glens Falls High School is involved in a hands-on activity. The boys wear suits and ties for a very formal look. From left to right are Louise Hitchcock, J. Ward Russell, Thomas Larkin, Wilbur Chambers, teacher Elizabeth Meserne, Walter Garrett, and Edward O. Blenis.

100

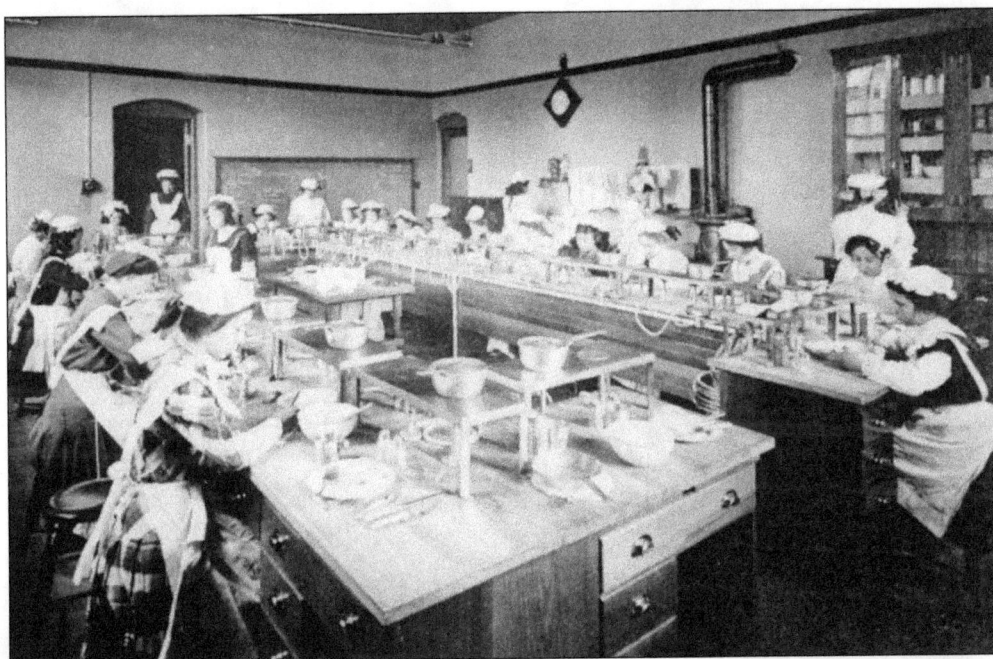

A HOME ECONOMICS CLASS, 1908. Glens Falls High School, on Glen Street, featured a specialized class for young ladies in domestic science (home economics). This class was for students who wished to move into a non-college, work-training program.

THE SOUTH STREET SCHOOL FACULTY, 1904. Women in high-necked blouses and long skirts reflect the fashion of the day in the teaching profession. The three teachers on the right in the back row wear glasses, with the one in the middle wearing pince nez, glasses that pinch on the end of the nose. Long hair piled high on the head was considered stylish on these unmarried teachers.

GLENS FALLS HIGH SCHOOL FOOTBALL, 1905. The high school football team had a very successful season in 1905. Here, nose guards hang around the necks of players and shin guards are worn, but their attire lacks uniformity. Identified in the photograph is freshman George Bayle, seated second from the right.

THE FOOTBALL SQUAD, 1921. The 1921 high school football team was undefeated, with only Saratoga scoring any points against them. Many on this team had names still existing in Glens Falls today, such as Wilcox, Akins, Potter, Dolan, Merrill, Allen, Sprague, Briggs, Varney, Tripp, Burns, and Davidson.

Six

TRANSPORTATION

A STAGECOACH, C. 1885. A coach traveling north on Glen Street is pictured in front of Union School No. 1, Glens Falls High School. Four matching horses pull a loaded coach. A gas street lamp sits at the side of the dirt street. Passengers riding inside paid premium rates and were protected from the elements. Top passengers had the advantage of fresh air but suffered the effects of bad weather and dust.

A HORSE-DRAWN CARRIAGE, C. 1890. A stately carriage with a "convertible" top waits in front of the Society of Friends church, on Ridge Street between Grand and Fulton Streets. The shock absorbers on each wheel made for a more comfortable ride for what must have been an affluent family.

A HORSE AND SLEIGH, C. 1890. In winter, sleighs were used, and horses wore special horseshoes with points for gripping the packed snow. Deep snow had to be removed from the streets, but a layer was left to be packed down so runners on winter vehicles could travel smoothly. Cold temperatures made riding in a "one-horse open sleigh" unpleasant.

A HORSE AND WAGON, C. 1885. This horse carriage holds a driver in front of the business of photographer Charles Oblenis, a contemporary of Seneca Ray Stoddard. The driver is unidentified, but the wagon could be a Joubert and White buckboard made in Glens Falls. The shock absorbers in front and back were a trademark of the company.

A DELIVERY WAGON, C. 1890. The Rochester Clothing Store (located first on the west side of Glen Street before 1890 and then in the YMCA building on the east side of the street) featured home delivery. A woman could go shopping and pick out something for her husband. She could then have it delivered to the home for fitting and final approval. The horse and wagon made deliveries possible.

A CLOSED DELIVERY CART, C. 1903. The Hovey Fruit and Ice Company was at 14½ Maple Street in 1901. Ice deliveries were needed every other day in homes, but stores like the Great Atlantic & Pacific Tea Company (A&P) on Ridge Street needed ice delivered daily. Fresh fruits and vegetables were also delivered to the stores. The horses have stringlike coverings that moved to help keep insects away.

A FARM WAGON, C. 1918. Farm wagons were used to bring goods to the Glens Falls train station for transport to markets out of the area. Here, chickens from the George Bayle Farm make their way to market. The traditional horse and wagon carried the goods to the more modern mode of transportation: the train.

A STEAM-POWERED ROAD-CONSTRUCTION VEHICLE, C. 1903–1910. The D. E. Van Wirt Construction Company was responsible for improving the roads in Glens Falls and laying the foundation for the Hudson Valley Railway Company. Here, the old and new come together on an area road.

THE RIDGE STREET FIRE STATION, C. 1900. The conversion of a barn enabled the completion of the Ridge Street Fire Station. The original building was torn down in 1939, and a new station was built on the northwest corner of Ridge and May Streets. In the middle cart are John Mack (left) and William Capron (right). The pumper driver is John Coffee, with John Bogart standing and Dan Murphy behind. The firemen on the left are unidentified.

A FIRE ENGINE, 1882. This is allegedly the first fire engine used in Glens Falls. The trap door on the top right opened so that the reservoir could be filled with water. The nozzle appears to be stationary, so aiming water at a fire was accomplished by positioning the cart.

A WINTER TROLLEY, C. 1885. The first trolleys were horse drawn and in winter were converted to sleighs. They did not run on tracks and held only seven passengers. The trolley pictured here is loading passengers at the rear of the car. The first Glens Falls Insurance Company building is in view on Glen Street. The conductor-driver stands in the open door at the front of the car.

ELECTRIC TROLLEYS, C. 1895. Summertime in Glens Falls allowed an open-air electric trolley to operate. The tracks seen here are on unpaved Glen Street. The second Glens Falls Insurance Company building can be seen between the trolleys. The second trolley is closed and is capable of being used in winter.

AN ELECTRIC TROLLEY, 1892. The trolleys had difficulty running in snow. The horse-drawn sleighs needed the snow to be packed down, while the trolleys needed it to be cleared. The snowbanks surrounding the car are near the Ferris and Viele drugstore (left) and the Stillwell and Allen hardware store (right) on Glen Street.

A TROLLEY CAR, C. 1897. The Glens Falls, Sandy Hill & Fort Edward Street Railroad Company began in 1885, connecting Glens Falls with the Bradley Opera House in Fort Edward. The trolleys were horse drawn at first, but by June 1891, electric cars were running the route. By 1897, more than 10½ miles of track were used by 18 cars. Doors were located at both the front and back of the car.

A LOCOMOTIVE, 1869. The railroad into Glens Falls was completed and a formal ceremony held on July 4, 1869. Fares were not charged on this day, so hundreds of families rode the train and even brought picnics to eat while traveling. The company operated 11 round trips between Glens Falls and Fort Edward, with a stop in Sandy Hill (Hudson Falls).

THE PASSENGER STATION, C. 1910. The Glens Falls Railroad Company began its connection with the outside world in 1869. It became the Rensselaer and Saratoga Company, which in turn became the Delaware and Hudson. By 1884, seven tracks ran into the Glens Falls terminal, reflecting the area's developing industries. The new station was completed and operational in 1897 at the corner of Lawrence and Cooper Streets. (Curran photograph.)

THE WATCHMAN'S SHANTY, C. 1910. Before the time of crossing gates at intersections, watchmen sat in small shanties waiting to step out and stop traffic when a train arrived. Here, a watchman sits at the shanty on East Hunter Street near Wing Street. (Curran photograph.)

THE TOLLBOOTH, C. 1890. This tollbooth was located at the north end of the village near Glenwood Avenue. Coaches and wagons were expected to pay a toll that supported maintenance of the dirt highway. In time, the road became a plank road, helping vehicles in the muddy seasons but providing an extremely bumpy ride.

A DELIVERY TRUCK, C. 1905–1910. O. C. Smith ran a grocery store at 178 Glen Street, No. 5 in the Crandall Block. Deliveries were made with this early truck. The vehicle lacked windows and doors but had roll-down flaps along the roof to use during inclement weather. Open-air vehicles like this one were impractical for winter use.

A MOVING VAN, OCTOBER 27, 1913. In this picture, furniture from a house fire on October 19, 1913, sits on a truck in front of the Glens Falls Insurance Company. The shock absorbers visible at the front are similar to those used on wagons and coaches. There are no windows or doors, and the steering wheel is on the right side. The men appear dapper in their hats and suits.

113

AN EARLY AUTOMOBILE, C. 1900. With mass production of automobiles, more and more people could afford to buy them. Because cars were able to travel up to 10 miles per hour, women had to tie down their hats. Shock absorbers at the front end made the ride smoother. Two jump seats are visible between the front and back seats. Note that there is no door for the front seat and the steering wheel is on the right side.

A FIRE TRUCK, C. 1909. An early fire truck in Glens Falls had no doors or roof. Built from a Buick touring car chassis, the box body held 300 feet of hose. It was used to haul coal for the Clapp and Jones steamer (a steam-powered fire truck). It was used in only two or three fires before being sold.

114

Seven

RECREATION, LEISURE, AND SPECIAL EVENTS

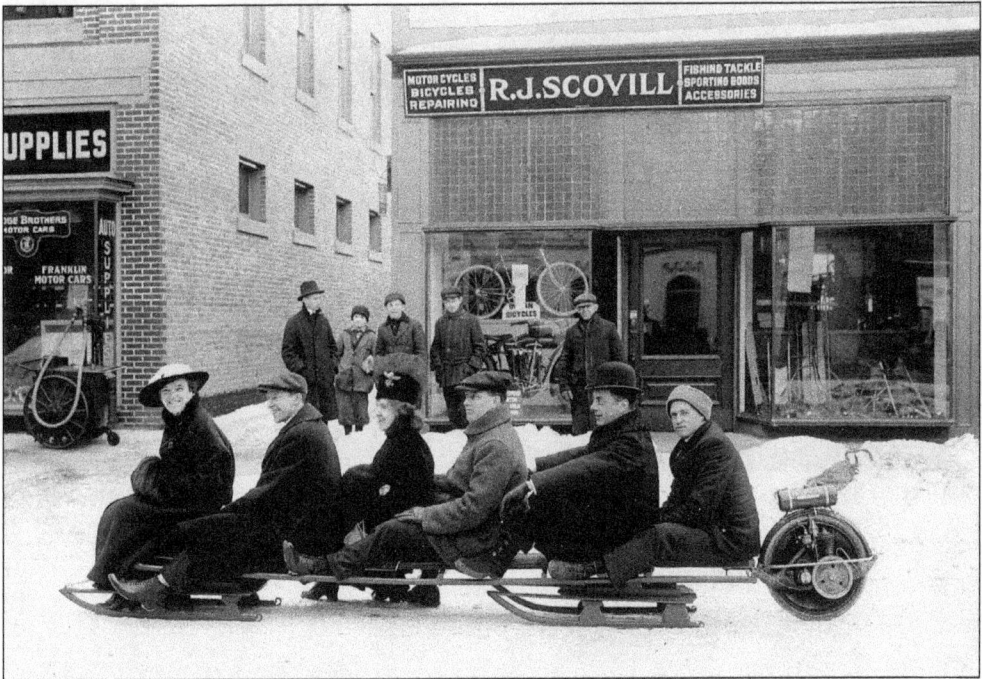

ADULTS HAVING FUN, 1916. A group is able to enjoy the snow on Ridge Street by riding on a powered sled. The store pictured here featured sporting goods and motorcycles and made general repairs to the same. The building next-door was the H. A. McRae and Company auto accessories store, currently Fiddleheads Restaurant. Even while participating in an outdoor sport, the women wore fashionable hats.

FISHING, 1898. Piers were placed in the Hudson River to allow lumbermen to sort the floating logs according to ownership. Boys took advantage of their location during the off-season to fish.

CHILDREN HAVING FUN, 1881. Children created their own fun. Boxes, tubs, and cradles became vehicles to paddle down a flooded, icy Elm Street. The reflections in the water here make an interesting composition. As with any unusual activity, an audience is drawn to the experience.

A PLAYGROUND, C. 1885. Children enjoy the slide on a playground. Knickers and hats on the boys, dresses on the girls, and high-button shoes are the fashion of the day. The umbrellas appear to be used for protection from the sun rather than rain.

THE CENTENNIAL CELEBRATION, 1913. A huge crowd gathers to hear Gov. William Sulzer speaking on August 6, near the Civil War Monument at the intersection of Glen and Bay Streets. On August 17, 1913, eleven days later, with less than one year in office, Sulzer was impeached.

THE GLENS FALLS CITY BAND, C. 1885. The Glens Falls City Band was preceded by a French cornet band (1881–1883). The band entertained in Glens Falls and surrounding areas.

WELCOME HOME, 1863. In this photograph, the Defiance Engine Company No. 1 lines Warren Street to welcome home Civil War soldiers whose enlistments expired on June 6, 1863. One of the early pumpers is parked on the dirt street under the elegantly decorated welcome arch.

THE CAST, 1888. The Glens Falls Opera House, on Warren Street, was home to activities in addition to opera. These students from the Glens Falls Academy participated in a class play in the opera house. Seated are Rachael Cookson (left) and Edith Fowler. In the back row are, from left to right, Fred DeVall, Jack Cahoan, Henry Cronkite, Lena Thompson, Mabel Cowles, and D. J. Eddy.

THE EMPIRE THEATER, C. 1900. The Empire Theater opened at 11–13 South Street in 1899. It held two concert halls, a lecture hall, several dancing halls, a banquet room, and an opera house with seating for 1,200 people. The basement contained a billiard room. On the third floor was a large ballroom. Vaudeville players who entertained here included George M. Cohan, Al Jolson, Ethel and Lionel Barrymore, and Harry Lauder. The theater later became a movie house. It closed its doors in July 1950 and was renovated into an office building.

FEEDING THE PIGEONS, C. THE 1920S. Two unidentified young ladies take time to feed the pigeons at the corner of Ridge and Glen Streets.

GLENS FALLS CITY PARK, 1920. This is a promotional picture taken for the Boy Scouts in Crandall City Park. Shown at the top right is Stephen Birdsall, son of Dr. Edgar Birdsall. At one time, City Park was lined with private residences, but the homes were removed so the new library could be built, and the park developed.

A PICNIC IN COLE'S WOODS, 1901. Sitting on a fallen tree across a stream, a group enjoys a day in Cole's Woods. Even during an outing, women wear long skirts, high-button shoes, and long-sleeved blouses. Named, but with no order given, are Miss Biers, Miss Abbott, Mabel Larno, Flora Larno, Lydia Brown, Florence Hanland, Eliza Stearns, Elsie Streeter, Edith Streeter, Leslie Stearns, Allan Stearns, Albert Curtis, and Tracy Brenan.

BOXING, C. 1895. A beach on the Hudson River was the site of a boxing match, despite the lack of a ring or referee. Spectators are well dressed for this summertime activity.

A BICYCLE RACE, C. 1880. Bicycle racing was a popular sport at a racetrack in Glens Falls. The track served the thoroughbred racing industry in town. The half-mile track was located on the northwest end of town, with a practice oval nearby. A hotel on Sanford Street, where the school is now located, accommodated the clientele visiting the facility.

A BICYCLIST, C. 1900. During the transition from horse and wagon to motorcars, bicycles were an important part of life in Glens Falls. Bicycle racing took place in the Glens Falls Opera House. Knickers were made for bicycle riding.

THE YMCA, C. 1925. In this photograph, a Glens Falls High School gym class meets at the YMCA. (The high school lacked a gymnasium until 1926.) Bloomer-style shorts, high-top footwear and knee socks were the uniform. Indian Clubs were used as part of an exercise program required by New York State curriculum.

CRANDALL PARK IN WINTER, 1915. With Glen Street in the background, skaters take advantage of ice on the ponds at Crandall Park. Boys wear knickers, and girls wear skirts.

FLAG DAY, C. 1890. Students prepare for a patriotic celebration at the Ridge Street School, on the corner of May and Ridge Streets. High-button shoes were the fashion for all. Boys wear knickers and knee socks. A gas chandelier hangs from the center of the room. A group photograph was a novelty at that time, although no one seems to be smiling about it.

A RED CROSS SHIPMENT, C. 1918. Seventh- and eighth-grade boys pose in front of the Glens Falls Junior High School, on Glen Street, with Red Cross packages to support troops in World War I. Third from the right on the ground is Foster Rhodes. Eleventh from the right is Francis Forbes.

THE CRANDALL PARK CANNON, C. 1910. A cannon graces the grounds of Crandall Park on upper Glen Street. In the middle is Bernice Millard Ball, and on the right is Pearl Cowan Ball of Ogden Street.

CRANDALL PARK, 1915. Gardens were among Henry Crandall's priorities in developing Crandall Park. The Neptune fountain was moved from downtown in 1898, and an obelisk, with his log mark on top, contained the graves of Henry Crandall and his wife. His matched pair of white horses is allegedly also buried nearby. The park is a quiet place to escape the busy downtown.

CRANDALL PARK, C. 1900. Henry Crandall purchased land from Cole's Woods in order to provide the community with a place for children to play. Trees and gardens were planted. Ponds were dredged and stocked with fish. A dirt road ran through the park so wagons could traverse its lands.

CRANDALL PARK LAKE, C. 1910. When Henry Crandall developed the park, one pond was so large that a motor launch operated on it. A dam was built to deepen the waters so "boys" could swim.